The principal objective of THE MATHESON TRUST is to promote the study of comparative religion from the point of view of the underlying harmony of the great religious and philosophical traditions of the world. This objective is being pursued through such means as audio-visual media, the support and sponsorship of lecture series and conferences, the creation of a website, collaboration with film production companies and publishing companies as well as the Trust's own series of publications.

The Matheson Monographs cover a wide range of themes within the field of comparative religion: scriptural exegesis in different religious traditions; the modalities of spiritual and contemplative life; in-depth mystical studies of particular religious traditions; broad comparative analyses taking in a series of religious forms; studies of traditional arts, crafts and cosmological science; and contemporary scholarly expositions of religious philosophy and metaphysics. The monographs also comprise translations of both classical and contemporary texts, as well as transcriptions of lectures by, and interviews with, spiritual and scholarly authorities from different religious and philosophical traditions.

THE LIGHT ALONE

THE LIGHT ALONE

Poems of Lalla Yogeshvari

∾

Rendered into English

by

Barry McDonald

THE MATHESON TRUST
For the Study of Comparative Religion

This first English edition published by

The Matheson Trust
PO Box 336
56 Gloucester Road
London SW7 4UB, UK

www.themathesontrust.org

ISBN: 978-1-908092-24-3

British Library Cataloguing-in-Publication Data.
A catalogue record for this book is
available from the British Library.

Typesetting, cover art and design by Susana Marín

CONTENTS

In memory of Sharlyn

INTRODUCTION[1]

L alla Yogeshvari (ca. 1320-1392) is beloved as a great saint in her native Kashmir and her verses have been memorized and treasured for more than 600 years by both Hindus and Muslims, especially the Sufis who recognize much of their traditional lore in her writings. According to Kamalakar Mishra of Benares Hindu University, Kashmir Shaivism is the central philosophy of Tantra, and an in-depth study of its doctrines and methods would bear much fruit in helping readers who wish to expand their knowledge of the context of Lalla's poems. In brief, Kashmir Shaivism, like Advaita Vedanta, presents a doctrine of non-dualism; its central tenet is the ultimate unity of the individual soul (*jiva*) with the immanent Self (Shiva). Concerning the concept of *Maya*, which is a critically important part of Hindu thought, Vedanta places the stress on *Maya* as illusion, that radiating power of creation which veils the Real; whereas Tantra views *Maya* more as *Lila*, the divine play by which the Real unveils itself in creation. Perhaps this difference of perspective is in the nature of *Maya*, ever-changing and elusive, escaping final definitions. It has been said that knowing *Maya* is like trying to examine darkness with a torch. Another important consideration, according to Mishra, is that Tantra views

---

[1] First published as "The Light Alone: Poems of Lalla Yogishwari", rendered into English by Barry McDonald, *Sacred Web* 16, Winter 2005.

undifferentiated, pure Consciousness, not as the stream but as the dynamic principle of Ultimate Reality, the *Shakti*, or creative power of Shiva. Consequently, because this Consciousness permeates all creation, the Tantric vision sees God everywhere. This vision is at the heart of Lalla's poetry.

Underlying a key difference between Shankara (ca. 788-820), the great exponent of Advaita Vedanta, and Avinabhagupta (ca. 975-1025), who is the comparable figure in Kashmir Shaivism, Frithjof Schuon observes that Advaita Vedanta proceeds by way of elimination, while Tantra proceeds by way of sublimation. Very broadly speaking, this is the difference between the apophatic and the cataphatic ways of negation and affirmation; apparently opposing viewpoints which like two lines arc in opposite directions but meet in closing the circle of the Oneness of God. Schuon writes: "Thus the symbolist mentality can be a unilateral tendency of the intelligence and the sensibility, but it can also be a spiritual realism on the plane of phenomena, in which case it gives rise to a sanctity based, not on negation, reflection and sacrifice, but on the concrete analogy between earthly phenomena and heavenly archetypes. This is the distinction between a Shankara and an Avinabhagupta or a Krishna, or between a Desert Father and David or Solomon; what is involved is not the cosmic scope of the holy personages, but only their manner of combining their already heavenly stations with the phenomena of earthly life."

One of the reasons for the enduring popularity of Lalla's poems, which are at once sober and ecstatic, echoing both *via negativa* and *via affirmativa*, is found in her remarkable ability to combine metaphysical doctrine with imagery drawn from everyday life. This occurs as a result of intense spiritual practice, transforming and refining the soul, causing the eye of the heart to open upon a purified and ennobled vision of the world where the physical and metaphysical are mutually reflected in each other. This alchemy, transmitted in part through her verses, allows readers with similar vision from different walks of life and various religious traditions, across six centuries and beyond the borders of her native Kashmir, to appreciate the great depth of her realization. The directness, simplicity, and clarity of Lalla's language reflect the spiritual poverty much loved by the Sufis; her words are windows through which shines the light of the knowledge of God. Her spare language is full of silence and her poems are like reverberations of the *japa-yoga* to which she often refers. This silence is also manifest in her *avadhuta* state; she has cast off all outwardness and trappings of custom; and this is the meaning of her naked dance. Realizing a spiritual station beyond sectarian differences and theological dispute, she is established in the Truth of truths. Schuon writes: "Sacred nudity—in India for example—expresses the exteriorization of that which is most interior; 'and that is why, naked, I dance,' as Lalla Yogeshvari said after having realized the immanent Self. Extremes meet; the natural form can be the vehicle of the supernatural essence, and the latter can be manifested by the former." The interiorization of the exterior, seeing God everywhere as a result of the metaphysical transparency of phenomena; and the exteriorization of the interior, the manifestation of the inmost Self, is a concise expression of the essence of Kashmir Shaivism. For Lalla, this expression is made manifest through her verses and dance.

The following selection of Lalla's verses is largely based upon the translation of Sir Richard Carnac Temple, entitled *The Word of Lalla: the Prophetess*, published by Cambridge University Press in 1924, and I humbly acknowledge my enormous debt to his monumental effort, especially during a time when such poetry must have seemed terribly strange to many scholars and poets in the

West. My sincere appreciation and gratitude must also be extended for the pioneering achievement of Sir George Grierson and Lionel D. Barnett whose book *Lalla-Vakyani, or the Wise Sayings of Lal Ded*, published by the Royal Asiatic Society of London in 1920 preceded Temple's translations and commentaries. Both volumes still have much to offer concerning the details of Lalla's poetry and thought. Being drawn for many years to Lalla's poems and to doctrines which resonate with her teachings, I have composed these revised versions with a hope that they may be of interest to new readers.

References and Suggestions for Further Reading:

Lalla-Vakyani, or the Wise Sayings of Lal Ded by Sir George Grierson and Lionel D. Barnett, (Royal Asiatic Society, 1920)

The World of Lalla, the Prophetess by Sir Richard Carnac Temple, (Cambridge University Press), 1924)

Kashmir Shaivism: The Central Philosophy of Tantrism by Kamalakar Mishra, (Rudra Press, 1993)

Roots of the Human Condition by Frithjof Schuon, (World Wisdom, 1991)

The Play of Masks by Frithjof Schuon, (World Wisdom, 1992)

THE LIGHT ALONE

Why cool a fire? Why stop a stream?
Why walk feet upwards in the sky?
Why milk a bull? Why magic dreams?
Why tricks of jugglers try?

Again born in this world to be,
The Light alone can liberation give.
What matter death takes me or thee?
Happy to die, we are content to live.

Lalla knows a lake so small

It cannot hide a mustard seed;

But mighty it appears withal,

Its waters fill a whole world's need.

Where mustard seed can't hide

A great rhinoceros may drink;

And where leviathan abides

One minnow fills up to the brink.

All day and night the elephant and deer

Drink from this lake of earth;

And meet like children of the year—

Death follows on the heels of birth.

A vision formed before my eyes,
Framed in a ring of burning thought;
Up to the heights, lo! I arise,
In God alone my soul was caught.

On wings of thought, my steed,
I rode through mists of evening gold;
Ascending higher still I speed
And there the Self I did behold.

Truth clad the naked body that is I;
Girt me about with flaming sword.
Robed in the infinite blue sky;
This garment is the glory of the Lord.

With laughter filled, or full of yawns,

Between a cough or sneeze,

Even in breath if sighs are drawn,

He shall be near in such as these.

By keeping an ascetic rule,

Or roaming naked through the year,

Or bathing in the holy pools:

Heed Him. In every action He is near.

A holy man roams place to place,

Seeks union with God.

Is He not now before thy face?

What good seeking Him abroad?

Discern the Secret in thy soul,

Have faith the Self in self to see.

Further thou art from what is Whole,

The more the world appeals to thee.

Keeping the disciplines of breath aright,

Touched not by thirst or hunger of the earth,

At end of life, absorbed in Light,

He knows good fortune in the world of birth.

Not by good attitude,

Nor ardent wish for peace;

Not by ego which intrudes

Shalt thou attain Release.

Like salt melts in the sea,

As body melts in thought;

If heart not by the Truth is taught

The Truth one knows, one cannot be.

The lake of nectar Lalla stirs,

With waves of union for her bed;

What is this passing life for her?

While in this life she's also dead.

Dead to all hope of thought and strife,

She dwells with the Supreme;

And free from death and birth and life:

Consciousness awakened in a dream.

Dark demons of temptation fly

From souls full of desire—

With Knowledge strike them till they die,

Or be consumed in fire.

For them a poison is true thought,

Feed them, therefore, the finest flour—

It bakes to bread by meditation taught;

Then know how small the demon's power.

"Think not on things without,
Fix on the inmost Self thy thought:
So shalt thou free thyself from doubt"—
These are the precepts that my Guru taught.

Dance, Lalla, clothed by the air:
Sing, Lalla, clothed in the sky.
Air and sky: what garment is so fair?
Custom says "cloth", but does cloth sanctify?

Beware unguided thoughts,

They fall to evil ways;

In consciousness of God is sought

The Truth no wickedness dismays.

Like suckling child that rests

On mother that he holds so dear;

Be thou of courage, without fear,

And snuggle close between her breasts.

I found deep in the soul,

A Moon of Knowledge bright.

In its clear light I learned the whole;

The Truth shall like with like unite.

Narayan, all is Thou;

In all, Narayan, only Thee,

O Naran, all play seen now—

Like rolling waves far out at sea.

I knew my Self the Self-Supreme,

I knew the world as sport;

I solved the riddle of the dream;

I knew the two in one Self consort.

By highway of Release I came,

From it I did not go.

I stumbled on the bridge of fame,

Lost time for what I did not know.

Fell in the stream of death, I found

Nothing to pay the ferry fee;

Not one coin, looking around,

Not Hari's Name to rescue me.

Birth in a woman's womb for me

Was useful as an empty dream.

So birth from woman is for thee—

Gain then the Truth of Self-Supreme.

By concentrated thought

Om and breath under control,

My mind in holy fire is caught,

My body like a blazing coal.

All places that there are in me,

All seats of action and their ways,

I conquered one by one till free;

Inside the point of Light I stayed.

Fill days and nights with cares of life,

Yet freedom in inaction find—

All actions from the cares of strife,

They cloud the mirror of the mind.

By learning Wisdom clouds shall clear;

Then gain the treasure of the Call;

Hearing the Call, know Self is near—

What art thou? Nothing. He is all.

No Knowledge just by work,

But on the road of pain;

No seeker off that road may walk,

To seek elsewhere he seeks in vain.

When I was It, though It was I,

I reached the Place of Wine—

Wine flows where *sahasrara* lie;

Abode of Bliss outside of time.

Who shall the rider be, if steed
Shiva, Self-Intelligence, shall be?
Who but Vishnu to attend His need?
And Brahma joins the Three.

If Self-Intelligence is I,
I Self-Intelligence must be.
Need two in One to mount Him by,
What rider but the One is He.

This Knowledge Lalla knows
When intuitions of the Self begin.
She hears a Sound that ever grows
Round point of Light she sees within.

Whatever work I did,

Whatever word I said—

That was the worship in my body hid,

That was the worship hidden in my head.

In consciousness of God awake

With spiritual eye I saw the dream;

No work or word could take away

My life absorbed in the Supreme.

THE RIDDLE

A sword a kingdom gains,

And merit profits thee—

In time Heaven is won by pain,

And Paradise by charity.

But still they cannot save thy soul;

Exhausted merit brings rebirth.

He's saved alone that learns control—

And follows Knowledge while on earth.

Virtue's harvest and the weed of vice,

They come from sowing seeds;

One from benefit, one from price—

Both gain and loss come from his deeds.

With yearning eyes,

Looked night and day,

Till I beheld the One, the Wise,

And seeing Him, He filled my gaze.

In daylight shone my lucky star:

Breathless, I held my Guide to be.

My Lamp of Knowledge blazed afar,

Fanned by every breath I breathed.

My soul now to the Self revealed,

All eyes could see my inner Light.

And though in darkness world was sealed,

I knew He was the Truth, and held Him tight.

Not I nor Thou;

Nothing to think, no thought—

Only the All-Creator, now

Mind forgotten in the Naught.

The hidden meaning in this dream,

Escaping ignorance in thought,

Except they see the All-Supreme,

And vanish in the Naught.

So many worlds are gone from them,

Release comes to the soul.

Through eyes of faith no longer dim—

The body lost, the mind made whole.

Keep little raiment for the cold,
Little food for stomach's sake.
Scraps for crows the body holds,
Mind a house of Knowledge make.

No final peace in rich attire,
Nor sweets shall satisfaction give.
Neither escapes from Yama's ire,
If like slaves of desire you live.

Who are the ones that flowers bring?

What flowers at the feet they lay?

What water on the image fling?

What is the spell Shankar shall sway?

Pure concentration flowers bring;

Flowers of fervent faith they lay.

Nectar of moon on Him they fling;

Their silence is the Word they pray.

Who is the one wrapped in sleep?
And who in wakefulness remains?
One mind in deepest slumber keeps;
One mind to wakefulness attains.

There is a world thou must rout,
So mind's self to the Self transcends.
The soul is ringed with things about,
For all men time comes to an end.

See space with its horizons deep,
And all experience life makes;
While fighting lasts the mind's asleep;
With fighting done the Self awakes.

.

O restless soul, fear not thy part,

Who was, and is, shall ever be—

What thou must do and where thou art,

Dwell where thou will, He thinks of thee.

He shall feed thee and keep thee clad,

Not rites or service be thy aim;

Neither a sacrifice to make Him glad,

Cry *Om* aloud, and His love claim.

With a scrap of thin thread

I tow my boat over the sea.

Will God hear prayers I have said?

And will He safely carry me?

Like wine in cup of unbaked clay,

Whirling it spills my dizzy soul.

In time the clay must melt away—

How joyful now to reach my goal!

Why twist a rope of sand?

Why tow with such a line?

How shall the boat come to thy hand?

To tow thou must make stronger twine.

Has not Naran written thy fate?

No one, Good Sir, shall alter His decree.

Only thine efforts may create

The union between Self and thee.

They come and go,

Night and day, always on and on,

Returning whence they came, and so

Wandering the universe, they're gone.

Weary, ceaseless, the unending round—

Birth, and birth again, in pain—

As every self on self rebounds

Naught follows naught, then naught again.

By consciousness of yogic art

From the dark cavern where it lies,

And through the life within the heart

Nothing but *Om*, the Spell of spells, may rise.

By yogic art transported to the Place

Om grows to unobstructed Sound,

What need is there to seek for grace

When in thy Self the Spell of spells is found?

He is the all-pervading One, the Lord;

The taintless One is one with thee.

If thou will learn this of thine own accord

What has been learned, so shall thou be.

Choose married life, choose hermitage,

Choose a pursuit that pleases thee.

If with desire thy heart does not engage,

What has been learned, so shall thou be.

Dwelling in thy mother's womb,

Thy vow was to be born no more.

Losing the wonder of that tomb,

What is recalled of days of yore?

If from rebirth thou would be free,

Die to desire, though death is still in store—

Great honor then is won by thee;

With Him in union evermore.

While hidden Thou remained
Since in Thyself Thou stayed absorbed;
Sight of Thy form I could not gain,
Since clay my form was covered o'er.

Until I knew that we were one,
All day I sought for Thee in me;
While clay lay drying in the sun,
All day I searched through clay to see.

And when I found that we were one,
I danced in joy, free from rebirth—
So seeing clay dry in the sun,
I knew Thee in all things on earth.

Lalla solved the riddle of the earth;
Heedless of her body's strength—
Nothing was her labor worth,
It's on the Author she would gaze at length.

And struggling, the door was tight,
Bolted and barred, yearning all the more
Him to behold—beyond her sight,
But she gazed only at the door.

And while she stood, before the door,
Centered on Him with all her soul,
Behold! He opened it forevermore;
And there, within herself, she saw Him whole.

THE MILLER

Without a thought of self,
A man sweats night and day—
His thought and labor not for wealth;
Hope for the fruits he's put away.

And if he calls on Shiva's Name,
The Sacred Way ever in mind,
Shiva and soul, two are the same—
"I am He" and "He is I" shall find.

Whoso shall find the two in One,
Let him then reap what work affords—
On him shines the all-gracious Sun;
The Lord of all the greatest lords.

Whatever work in which I toil,

Burdens on me lie;

Yet to another falls the spoil—

He gains the fruit, not I.

But working with no thought of self;

All works before the Self I lay.

Place faith and duty before wealth,

And travel well along the way.

Not name, nor line, nor form, nor hue,

Has unobstructed Sound;

Who of Himself, the empty blue,

What home but in the Void is found?

His own reflection is the Morn,

And His supremacy the Fount;

Who with the Absolute, the Void adorned,

The Self is steed, and thou shalt mount.

Forever new, the story of a soul,

Forever changed from birth to birth;

And so the moon that waxes whole

Grows new again each month on earth.

Forever new, the universe dissolved,

A flood of waters on the earth;

From flood of waters new resolved

The world came forth again to birth.

With body cleansed, and with clear mind,

Ever anew Lalla has grown.

A vision now that once was blind,

And Knowledge then had nothing known.

Keep wealth and kingdom, live
Bowed with care, bent by desire.
Thy riches to another give,
The heart in discontent is mired.

The soul that from desire is free,
It is detached from all of this;
Learn death in life, true Life to be,
Knowledge of Truth alone is Bliss.

Think till the light of day
Is like the darkness of the night—
Till Self-Illuminated way
Reveals the darkness is the light.

Consumed by fire of Love,
My Knowledge passes how and why:
And dwelling in the Void above
The two in One: The Self and I.

By mystery of yogic art

The steed of thought speeds in the sky;

And in the blinking of an eye

It finds the heaven of the heart.

By rein of breath-control,

Breathless, I'll guide thee ways I know;

My chariot of Knowledge rolls

And down the paths of Self I go.

Rise, Lady, offer to the Name—

Bear in hand the flesh and wine;

In offering no loss or shame,

Though not a custom that is thine.

When Knowledge of the Truth is found

A loud cry of awakening is heard—

A unity between the Lord and Sound,

And Sound united with the Word.

I, Lalla, cotton bloom,

Set forth on path of life;

But then the knocks of cleaning room,

And hard blows of carder's wife.

Fine thread from me a woman spun;

She twisted me upon her wheel.

Then on her loom I was undone;

Nothing but weaver's kicks could feel.

Cloth now become, on washing stone,

Till washer man was satisfied.

He whitened me with earth, skin and bone,

Till in the wonder of the Self I died.

Thou heedless one, set forth with speed;

Follow thy journey to its end.

Gain Knowledge, there's no other need—

Now dawn has broken, seek thy Friend.

For shoes place wings upon thy feet;

This ocean has no bridge to lend.

Take flight; this world is dust and sleet—

Now dawn has broken, seek thy Friend.

I filled my goblet to the brim,

With wine of words that favor gives;

I drained the cup till eyes grew dim;

In drunkenness awhile I lived.

Yet from the cup I sought no prize;

In it I never placed my trust.

And still it helped to clear my eyes—

Wine purified them of world's dust.

Strong is the courage of my wine,

I seized the curtain and tore it away—

Before me then was path divine,

And nothing more to cloud my way.

A heavy bag upon my back;

Sling and knot my shoulders gall.

My back is crooked now, alas!

How can I bear it? I must fall.

My Guru found, I heard him tell

The Truth blistered my heart.

Illusions pain, loved so well;

How can I bear it? I must fall.

Now flock of thoughts are lost;

The shepherd gone beyond recall.

Now mountain of Release to cross—

How can I bear it? I must fall.

Keep mind calm as a peaceful sea,

Extinguish fire of wrath—

Lest from thy bondage thou set free

Words of rage, like flames, burst forth.

These words, searing the mind,

Are burned in anger, healed in truth.

What are these words? Just wind

When weighed upon the scale of Truth.

When one asks aught of thee, say "yes";

When someone speaks, to listen feign;

When one exhorts, his keenness bless,

And depth and height of Knowledge gain.

Thou the Heavens, Thou the earth:

Thou the day and night and air:

Thou all things that may give birth,

Thou the flowers fair.

Thou the sacrificial meal,

Thou the water poured on Thee:

Thou the medicines that heal.

Need Thou offering from me?

How came I here? And by what road?

Where shall I go, and by what way?

Both Thou and I in one abode:

Like empty breath I pass my day.

If heart pays heed

To all thy Guru teaches thee,

Thy worship then no water needs,

Nor garland, grass, no sesame.

Shiva then shall meditation gain

By loving yearning of the heart.

On heights of joy thou shall remain

And be with Him in lover's part.

From every action soul set free,

No fear of living or rebirth—

Alone with the Supreme to be

Free from the trials of this earth.

Once swan-like, my voice divine;

Now I have sung, my voice is mute—

Something stolen that was mine;

The thief I do not know, nor dispute.

My mill is stopped, choked with grain—

The grain offered to Miller wise.

I've sung but will not sing again

For now the Miller is before my eyes.

Are not all idols lumps of stone?
Aren't stone the temples thine?
Venerable Brahman, why alone
Offer to these to make divine?

Hold breaths that in thy body rise
And meditate upon the One alone;
So thou be understanding, wise,
And know that He is not of stone.

Water, snow, and ice: these three

Separate seem—

They are the same to eyes that see

By one light: Consciousness Supreme.

What cold divides, sun combines.

What sun divides, Shiva makes whole.

What Shiva parts, the Absolute defines

In unity: Shiva, universe, and soul.

A BUBBLE ON THE WIND

Shall little ash a mirror stain?

Shall little word a heart distress?

Shall little goading service strain?

How shall the Lord His adepts bless?

Hast knowledge, be a fool;

Hast vision, now be blind.

Hast hearing now, let deafness rule,

And of all thought empty thy mind.

A bubble on the wind shall ride;

Thy hands pluck wind up by the root.

A strand of hair an elephant to guide;

Water poured through straw is thy repute.

What wealth? Nothing in mind.

What action, or inaction, may intrude?

A vow of silence fails to find;

No use for mystic attitude.

Not even Shiva reigns supreme,

His *Shakti* holds no sway;

The unknown Void, beyond all dreams,

Pursuing an elusive way.

Finding peace in forest glade,

Some have abandoned home;

In home-life others peace have made,

They have no wish to roam.

What matter if beneath the sky

Or underneath a roof is home?

Stay where thou art, the Self is nigh,

In all who settle, all who roam.

With every trace of darkness gone,

Illusion vanished in the dawn;

In love of God, Lalla was glad

And love cured what had made her sad.

She cried to her Beloved: "It is I",

It's Lalla who awakens Thee.

Now buried in a crystal lake they lie,

Defilements that once darkened me.

"Self of myself, Thou art but I;

Self of myself, I am but Thou".

The two in One shall never die;

What does it matter, why and how?

Who sees the Lord of lords?

He from duality is free;

Seeing one Self in selves that be,

He knows that day and night accord.

Who is the man freed from rebirth?

He has the Knowledge and the Light.

Self-realized on earth,

On bliss of Self he sets his sight.

Who is the fool courting rebirth?

On ignorance he's set;

Adding to learning gained on earth

Knot after knot in tangled net.

Impurities that hinder thee,

Works that joy and pain may lend,

Appearances defining all we see,

Thought that the soul has an end.

All deeds, both good and bad,

Discern them by suspending breath;

So thou be neither sad nor glad,

This shall save from the fear of death.

Shall liberation then be thine;

Another world shall thee absorb.

In thee the Light of God shall shine—

Rise to the sun and pierce its orb.

Hast thou for chariot and throne

Royal emblems; the whirl

Revelry affords; and for thine own

Bewitching graces of a dancing girl?

Possess pillows of cotton down, all things

Which are luxurious? With final breath

What lasting comfort brings?

What saves thee from the fear of death?

Of Knowledge and of deeds,

Herbs in the garden grow.

Restraining fences round them throw,

Built by works, serving need.

Stakes of contemplation and control,

Ward off temptations round thee set;

And bars of rites to keep thy soul

Free from distractions in mind's net.

Keep clean the garden of thy heart,

So lilies may in blossom be.

And thou give answer for thy part

When like a Judge, Death questions thee.

Unto himself the Self is home—

He knows that Place to be a shrine—

There unobstructed Sound divine;

It rings eternally in vibrant *Om.*

When every vanity has fled,

Why trust in what shall come and go?

Why worship then by others led

When in thine heart the Self may know?

O holy *Siddh*, lend saintly ear,

Heed these poor words from me:

For many days thou lingered here,

Does memory profit thee?

O children, hearken unto me—

How pass your days and nights?

Dark, and darker, shall future be;

What shall ye do to seek the Light?

In future Nature will bow down

To them that walk in wrongful ways.

Autumn pears and apples ripen now;

Now ripen apricots of summer days.

In coming days of shame and wrath

Mother and daughter, hand in hand,

They will, approaching strangers, wander forth;

Women and men joined in an evil band.

Feed fatted rams, thou worldly one,

Take grains and sweets, then slay;

Leave every thought of "said and done",

Last fruits of learning cast away.

See with a spiritual eye the Place

Where the abode of God shall be:

There passes terrors of disgrace,

There custom loses hold on thee.

A dry leaf in the wind

I've seen a hungry wise man fall;

Winter's hunger claiming him, for all

The benefit could Wisdom find.

I've seen a rich and graceless fool

Beating his cook for meal's delay;

I'm waiting for the love and rule,

What binds me will be cut away.

Mind is a donkey; set it not free—

Rich saffron-gardens it devours;

And bringing on all ills that be,

Soon hear the tick: retribution's hour.

Let mind not stray from the fount

Knowledge gives to nourish it withal.

What has thou but donkey to mount?

It's on thy back that blows will fall.

Slay first the thieves—desire, lust, and pride;

Learn then to be the slave of all.

Thieves only for a time abide;

Forever lives the servant's Call.

All man gains here is nothing worth,

Save when his service is the sword;

The ash from fire is sun of birth;

Gain then the Knowledge of the Lord.

ABOUT THE AUTHOR

BARRY MCDONALD (1951-2021) is the author of *The Eagle's Flight* (Sophia Perennis, 2008) and *No Other Word* (The Matheson Trust, 2020). He is the editor of *Every Branch in Me: Essays on the Meaning of Man* (World Wisdom, 2002), *Seeing God Everywhere: Essays on Nature and the Sacred* (World Wisdom, 2003) and co-editor, with Patrick Laude, of *Music of the Sky: An Anthology of Spiritual Poetry* (World Wisdom, 2004). His writings have appeared in numerous journals in the US and abroad.

INDEX OF FIRST LINES

9 781908 092243